# CAREERS FOR YOUR CAT

# CAREERS FOR YOUR
# CAT

ann dziemianowicz

illustrations by ann boyajian

10
TEN SPEED PRESS
Berkeley

Published in the United States by Ten Speed Press,
an imprint of the Crown Publishing Group, a division
of Random House, Inc., New York.
www.crownpublishing.com
www.tenspeed.com

Ten Speed Press and the Ten Speed Press colophon
are registered trademarks of Random House, Inc.

Library of Congress Cataloging-in-Publication Data

Dziemianowicz, Ann.
  Careers for your cat / Ann Dziemianowicz ;
illustrations by Ann Boyajian.
      p. cm.
  1. Cats—Humor. I. Boyajian, Ann. II. Title.
  PN6231.C23D995 2010
  818'.607—dc22
                              2010002624

ISBN 978-1-58008-124-5

Printed in China
Cover and interior design by Betsy Stromberg
Cover illustrations by Ann Boyajian

10 9 8 7 6 5 4 3 2 1

First Edition

Disclaimer: The author regrets that her husband of thirteen years has developed a severe cat allergy. She can no longer be owned by a cat and must live vicariously through her clients. Her husband is now in the doghouse.

To Mary, my lil' sister, and John, my lil' brother—I look up to you both.

. . . . . . . . . . . . .

And in memory of Mom, who inspired me, and Dad, who could tell a story. Love you.

. . . . . . . . . . . . .

To Bibsy, Fella, and Milton, my kitties, who taught me everything I know and achieved everything I dreamt for them.

# CONTENTS

· · · · · · · · · · · · · · · · · · · ·

# INTRODUCTION

Dear Cat Owner:

I've seen it for far too many years. It's always the same scenario. You're toiling away at your job, putting in the overtime to bring home the bacon—and the Fancy Feast—and what is Fluffy, your freeloading, fat cat, doing?

Snoozing on the love seat?

Staring out the window?

Soaking in the sunlight?

I'll tell you what she *isn't* doing, she isn't raising one paw to help you. Nope. Your cat is watching TV, waiting for you to come home. This cannot go on.

Your cat needs to get off the couch and get a job. Right now!

I have over fifteen years experience as a life coach and career counselor, and I have dedicated my life's work to helping once-feckless felines find meaning in their nine lives through challenging and rewarding employment. My belief is that with the proper guidance, *all* cats can master the skills needed to reach their potential as fully contributing members of their households.

It began in the early 1990s when an economic recession put a dent in my lifestyle. Although I wanted to shield my sheltered kitties from the undignified reality of want ads, resumes, and interviews, my bank account was sucking wind. I had three hungry mouths to feed. What could I do? I propelled Fella, Bibsy, and Milton into the workforce. Fella went into law enforcement; Bibsy launched a successful catering business, and Milton pursued a long and varied career in the entertainment industry.

My methods work and because they do, I have numerous celebrity clients. I've personally counseled many of the cats you've seen in movies, television commercials, and print ads. My phone number is also on the speed dials of famous, once-frustrated cat owners across the country, and I have plans to take my message—and my business—global.

The thousands of cats I've coached through the years have thanked me for transforming their lives. Once unmotivated, underachieving, and entitled, my client roster now includes a rap artist with lucrative recording and endorsement contracts, a best-selling self-help author, and a highly visible White House staffer. To a feline, they have claimed nothing less than spiritual reawakening. No longer bored, overfed, and sluggish, they wake up in the morning refreshed and inspired to join the rat race.

Take Bubbles, a five-year old cream-colored Persian. Three years ago her owner (we'll call her "Kathy") called me, inconsolable. She explained that Bubbles was sleeping seventeen hours a day. Imagine that, doing nothing in your life but catching up on your beauty sleep? I invited them both to my office for a consultation.

Kathy, a slender, attractive woman in her midthirties, was a wreck. Nervous, with dark circles under her eyes, she had all the classic symptoms of caffeine overload. Bubbles, on the other hand, looked gorgeous, well rested, every hair in place, perfectly groomed. She wore a pink diamond collar that accentuated her limpid blue eyes. When Kathy started talking, Bubbles crossed her legs and yawned.

After listening to Kathy's story, I went straight to the heart of the matter: "The problem is quite severe. Bubbles needs to find work. She needs a purpose in life."

"What?" Kathy seemed shocked. "Bubbles, um, doesn't work."

The cat curled her tail into a question mark.

"You've been waiting on her since she was born?" I said.

"True, but . . . "

"She eats her meals off silver plate or fine china?" I questioned.

"Well, yes, because she refuses to eat off of anything else."

"You brush and comb her daily?"

"Well, sure, but——"

"And," I added, "you praise her constantly for doing . . . nothing?"

Kathy looked sheepish.

"You need to let go, Kathy. Bubbles should be supporting you. She is a very capable cat."

Kathy agreed to let me meet one-on-one with Bubbles for an in-depth personality assessment and subsequent career analysis.

First, Bubbles took the Meowers-Briggs Career/Personality Test to determine her career type. The Meowers-Briggs Test zeroes in on a cat's special personality traits—friendly or reserved, whimsical or serious, sensitive or self-confident. Once Bubbles pinpointed her type, I could help her gain a clear understanding of her abilities. From there, she could be steered toward a suitable selection of career choices.

Upon completing the test, Bubbles was excited to discover she was an Intellectual Extravert (an IE). Together we explored the countless career opportunities that a cat of her type would find satisfying. A steely resolve shone in her azure eyes, for years she had been underestimated. People had seen her beauty, but not her brains.

Bubbles is now a successful advertising executive in Manhattan. You'll find Kathy, who recently quit her job in publishing, living half the year in Turks and Caicos working on her tan. In fact, Bubbles has expressed concern about Kathy's lack of ambition. But that's for another book.

Although I have been a cat counselor in private practice for many years, this first consultation with Bubbles was a defining moment for me. I saw I had the ability to turn around a cat's life—and the life of the person who loved her. I realized I needed to share my experience and offer my services to other exhausted cat owners and their well-rested cats. So I wrote this book for you. It is the only career guide written exclusively for cats and their special needs.

This book will transform your cat's life—and yours, too. Look how my methods helped Jack.

A muscular tabby with a clipped ear, Jack enjoyed tearing up his home like a rebellious teen. He ripped up newspapers, broke costly knickknacks, overturned potted plants, shredded the furniture, and scattered kitty litter across the kitchen. It was easy to find him—all you had to do was follow his path of destruction.

When I managed to get Jack to sit down, I administered the Meowers-Briggs Test. As I suspected, he was a Labor-Intensive Introvert (an L-II). Jack is now working as a building contractor. He has since replaced the tattered wall-to-wall carpeting in his owner's house and added a new bathroom with a sunken spa tub.

In *Careers for Your Cat*, I've provided you with the same Meowers-Briggs Career/Personality Test that put Bubbles and Jack on the road to success. You can help your cat complete the quiz today so he can identify his unique personality type and find the job of his dreams. In addition, I have profiled thirty-five hot kitty career options. You'll also find a special bonus section of my own personal tips written just for your cat on acing the interview process.

Your feline *can* find personal fulfillment, even in today's challenging job market. You know you need this book.

So wake up that lovable, lounging slacker and tell him it's time he got a job. And maybe it's time for a catnap yourself.

—Ann Dziemianowicz, CCC

# THE MEOWERS-BRIGGS CAREER / PERSONALITY TEST:

## Part One

**P**art One of the test will determine your cat's Career Type. It's wise to administer this test after a meal in a distraction-free environment. Place your kitty cat in your lap. Encourage him or her to choose the *most accurate* answer for each question. If two options seem appropriate, your cat may select both, but it is not acceptable to select more than two options.

## 1. What is your favorite activity?

A ___ Anything that involves string: chasing it, sculpting it, guarding it, killing it.

B ___ Athletic activities: high jump, long jump, vaulting, tackling, or badminton.

C ___ Meowing, purring, socializing, or just hanging out where the people are.

D ___ Napping, hiding in cupboards or drawers, or curling up quietly where I won't be disturbed, for goodness sakes.

E ___ Riding in the car.

## 2. What do you enjoy playing with?

A ___ Nonstandard toys: paper bags, loose string, bottle caps, rubber bands, jewelry, or anything that looks interesting.

B ___ Other cats, or toys I can sink my teeth or claws into and pretend it's another cat. Grrr.

C ___ Catnip-filled or other mind-altering toys that allow me to expand my horizons, fuel the imagination.

D ___ Play? But that would involve getting up. No thanks.

E ___ People with Frisbees, balls, sticks.

## 3. Where do you prefer to sleep?

A ____ Thoughtfully chosen locations throughout the home for contrast of color (for example, dark fur on light-colored laundry), contrast of texture, or the sunniest spot, darling.

B ____ Anywhere challenging! No place is too high, low, or difficult to get to. Bring it on!

C ____ On top of books, newspapers, the mail, file folders, keyboards, school projects, laundry.

D ____ Nearest flat surface; doesn't matter as much as location, though commonly found often on sofas, chairs, and beds.

E ____ None of the above—would rather be awake than asleep, and probably outdoors.

## 4. When it comes to fine dining, you:

A ____ Insist on the pricey stuff, often specialty or organic. Prefer the single serving cans of moist food. Must be served at room temperature.

B ____ Prefer whatever cat food is available, the more the better. And for goodness sake, don't be late serving it.

C ____ Are discerning, but not overly fussy. No generic cheapo brands, but not a Fancy Feast fancier. Will eat either dry or wet food. No problem.

D ____ Doesn't matter so much, as long as it is dependable, and good enough to be worth the effort of getting up.

E ____ Like dog food, cat food, people food, table scraps, garbage, or just about anything. Whatcha got?

## 5. When a mouse runs by and disappears under the refrigerator, you:

A ___ Spend as many as twenty-four hours crouching by the fridge, visualizing all possible ways to get at it, or draw it out. Not above rearranging furniture to get to it.

B ___ Catch it and save it for dessert.

C ___ Befriend it, or at least am more interested in observing it than in eating it. Rodents are not one of the foods groups. Believe me.

D ___ What mouse? Isn't that your problem? Call the exterminator and leave me in peace.

E ___ None of the above.

## 6. What happens when food is placed in front of you?

A ___ Scratch at or pace around dish, maybe rearrange it, then eat. Will walk away if menu is not up to snuff.

B ___ Gobble it right up, usually without pause. Sometimes give a quick thanks when done.

C ___ Check to ensure that it indeed is the best thing being offered, then eat. Not above coming back later to finish it off.

D ___ Let it sit there until good and ready to get up and eat.

E ___ Eat mine, and yours, too, if given the chance.

## 7. When greeted by a dog, how do you react?

. . . . . . . . . . . . . . . . . . . . . . . . . . . . . . . . . . . . . . . . . . . . . . . . . . .

A ____ Eyeball the dog, might allow a sniff, but otherwise more concerned with getting back to being the center of attention in the room.

B ____ Show the dog who's boss. Have been known to hiss, swat, or show annoyance, if dog invades my personal space. Not at all afraid of the dog.

C ____ Sometimes rub against the dog, or exchange sniffs. Study dog from a distance, but most often decide that the dog is hardly worthy of further attention.

D ____ What dog? That thing? Oh please.

E ____ Run over and sniff its butt.

## 8. When a stranger enters your home, you:

. . . . . . . . . . . . . . . . . . . . . . . . . . . . . . . . . . . . . . . . . . . . . . . . . . .

A ____ Announce him/her in some way, then either stay in the center of the room to show off, or go from person to person.

B ____ Jump up on guest's lap or get physically affectionate right away. Push hard in response to a friendly petting. Purr loudly. This is the life, baby.

C ____ Are interested in the person, but want to make sure it's safe before jumping into the fray. Retreat on occasion. Sometimes more drawn to women or quieter people.

D ____ Don't move if in the same room, or decline to emerge if in another room.

E ____ None of the above.

## 9. What do you do in the quiet hours before bed?

A ___  Stay where the people are, making every social minute count.

B ___  Race around, getting a second wind of activity. Might request a final outdoor prowl and yowl before bed.

C ___  A thorough cleaning and contemplation on the day's passing, which can sometimes be mistaken for light napping. Take care of personal housekeeping.

D ___  Stay put, resting up for the long night's sleep ahead.

E ___  None of the above.

## 10. To show displeasure, you:

A ___  Find a way to express myself: hiss, yowl, knock things over to make sure there's no misinterpreting my displeasure.

B ___  Go into destructor mode, sometimes slipping into a kitty-sized rage: shredding, clawing, and other destructive activities.

C ___  Put the ears back and give you the silent treatment. Often retreat to think things over; nurse grievances.

D ___  Act blasé, nonplussed—who needs you anyway?

E ___  Displeasure? What's that? Never heard of it.

## 11. You spend hours staring out the window at:

A ____ Own reflection. May change position from time to time to calculate best angles.

B ____ Birds, cats, dogs, or other small mammals. Consider exactly how to catch, kill, maim, or open a can of whoop-ass on each one.

C ____ Nothing in particular. Enjoy the exercise of going into a Zen state. May follow movement, studying the mechanics of it.

D ____ Staring? That would require opening my eyes and paying attention to something.

E ____ Anything that looks like it could be my new best friend.

## 12. You respond best to:

A ____ Clean litterbox, or fresh pile of clean laundry.

B ____ Sound of the can opener, or a shaker of treats.

C ____ My people returning home.

D ____ Well-made bed, or an empty sofa cushion.

E ____ Car engine turning over.

## 13. You expect to be treated like:

**A** \_\_\_\_  Royalty.

**B** \_\_\_\_  A finely tuned specimen of physical perfection. Expect to have full run of house and property, and please, make sure dinner is served on time.

**C** \_\_\_\_  An equal member of the household.

**D** \_\_\_\_  An important, respected, and valued piece of art. It's better to be looked at and left alone, rather than touched.

**E** \_\_\_\_  None of the above.

## 14. You purr the loudest when:

**A** \_\_\_\_  Being groomed with a comb or brush; require close attention paid to the delicately rendered fur around ears and chin.

**B** \_\_\_\_  Receiving a deep tissue massage and the occasional vigorous scratching.

**C** \_\_\_\_  Receiving firm, continuous strokes from head to tail while listening to verbal appraisal of my good looks.

**D** \_\_\_\_  Why should I purr when you're the one getting all the pleasure?

**E** \_\_\_\_  Purr? Nah, I just drool to express my happiness.

## 15. You love friends who:

. . . . . . . . . . . . . . . . . . . . . . . . . . . . . . . . . . . . . . . . . . . . .

**A** ____ Bring gifts and/or make a big fuss over me.

**B** ____ Give a good scratching and smell interesting.

**C** ____ Have softer voices and don't speak to me in demeaning baby talk.

**D** ____ Don't expect me to move or otherwise disrupt my nap, wherever it is.

**E** ____ Come ready to play.

## 16. You come for dinner when:

. . . . . . . . . . . . . . . . . . . . . . . . . . . . . . . . . . . . . . . . . . . . .

**A** ____ You walk into the kitchen—you exist to serve me, remember?

**B** ____ The exact moment the clock hits dinner hour. I'm waiting.

**C** ____ When called or tempted by alluring aromas.

**D** ____ When good and ready. Sleeping comes before eating almost all the time.

**E** ____ It's always dinnertime.

## COUNT UP THE TOTAL NUMBER OF LETTERS:

Total As____

Total Bs____

Total Cs____

Total Ds ____

Total Es____

If your total has more As than any other letter, you have determined that your cat has **CREATIVE** traits. Go to page 18 and fill in the blank provided. Then administer Part Two of the test. Do not skip this step.

If your total has more Bs than any other letter, your cat has **LABOR-INTENSIVE** traits. Go to page 18 and fill in the blank provided. Then administer Part Two of the test. Do not skip this step.

If your total has more Cs than any other letter, your cat has **INTELLECTUAL TRAITS**. Go to page 18 and fill in the blank provided. Then administer Part Two of the test. Do not skip this step.

If your total has more Ds than any other letter, your cat may have trouble fitting into the normal working world. Your cat is an **INERT INTROVERT**, but don't worry, even Inert Introverts can find jobs and be useful members of the household. Go to page 80 for selected solutions.

If your total has more Es than any other letter . . . are you sure your cat isn't a dog?

If your total has a close or equal number of letters—then lucky you. Your cat is a polymath . . . a multitalented multitasker. There are many careers to choose from.

# THE MEOWERS-BRIGGS CAREER / PERSONALITY TEST:

## Part Two

**P**art Two of the test will indicate your cat's Personality Type. As with Part One, it's advisable to administer Part Two of the test in a distraction-free environment. Note that there can be only one appropriate answer to each question. Place your kitty in your lap and resume testing.

## PART A
*Answer Yes for true, No for false.*

**1. Given the option, you will be found out of the way, usually sleeping.**

____Yes   ____No

**2. You generally keep to yourself, except at mealtimes.**

____Yes   ____No

**3. You prefer to be left alone by strangers and guests.**

____Yes   ____No

**4. You prefer to nap in safe, dark places.**

____Yes   ____No

**5. You are seldom seen flopped in the middle of a room or doorways and are rarely underfoot.**

____Yes   ____No

**6. You prefer to sleep curled up, rather than sprawled out.**

____Yes   ____No

Part A Total Yes responses_____

## PART B
*Answer Yes for true, No for false.*

**1. You are an exuberant purrer, meower, or talker.**

\_\_\_Yes   \_\_\_No

**2. You enjoy climbing on furniture, shelves, desks, etc.**

\_\_\_Yes   \_\_\_No

**3. You are adventurous. If an indoor cat, you would be, if given the chance.**

\_\_\_Yes   \_\_\_No

**4. You live to be petted or stroked, perhaps going so far as to have your belly rubbed or scratched.**

\_\_\_Yes   \_\_\_No

**5. You are more often found around people, rather than hiding away in a corner.**

\_\_\_Yes   \_\_No


Part B Total Yes responses_____

Compare Part A to Part B. If you have more Yes responses to Part A then your cat is an **INTROVERT**. If you have more Yes responses to Part B then your cat is an **EXTRAVERT**. If both are equal, then your cat is a true middle-of-the-road kind of personality who will have twice the career choices!

## DETERMINING YOUR CAT'S CAREER TYPE

Part One _____

(results from Part One determine that your cat has Creative, Labor-Intensive, or Intellectual traits)

## DETERMINING YOUR CAT'S PERSONALITY TYPE

Part Two_____

(results from Part Two indicate that your cat is an Introvert or an Extravert)

Part One results + Part Two results =

_____

(Your Cat's Career/Personality Type)

Go to page 20 if your cat is a **CREATIVE EXTRAVERT**

Go to page 30 if your cat is a **CREATIVE INTROVERT**

Go to page 40 if your cat is a **LABOR-INTENSIVE EXTRAVERT**

Go to page 50 if your cat is a **LABOR-INTENSIVE INTROVERT**

Go to page 60 if your cat is an **INTELLECTUAL EXTRAVERT**

Go to page 70 if your cat is an **INTELLECTUAL INTROVERT**

Go to page 80 if your cat is an **INERT INTROVERT**

# CAREER OPTIONS

# CAREERS FOR THE CREATIVE EXTRAVERT (CE)

**CREATIVE EXTRAVERTS (CEs)** are gregarious night owls and always the life of the party. Occasionally, CEs have attitude problems and at times are extremely fussy. Creative Extraverts hold themselves, and especially those around them, to a higher standard and often find inspiration when in front of an audience.

Some top career choices include:

OPERA SINGER

. . . . . . . . . . . . . . . . . . . . . . . .

CHORAL DIRECTOR

. . . . . . . . . . . . . . . . . . . . . . . . . . . .

INTERIOR DESIGNER

. . . . . . . . . . . . . . . . . . . . . . . . . . . .

CELEBRITY PHOTOGRAPHER /
PHOTOJOURNALIST

. . . . . . . . . . . . . . . . . . . . . . . . . . . .

ART HISTORIAN / MUSEUM CURATOR /
GALLERY DIRECTOR

# OPERA SINGER

Strong vocal capabilities

Can hit the high notes

Comfortable with solos

Adores the spotlight

# CHORAL DIRECTOR

Physically expressive

Commanding presence

Excels at group vocals

Positive, can-do attitude

# INTERIOR DESIGNER

Able to make inventive fabric alterations

Flair for transforming any living space

Displays a flamboyant personal style

Can deconstruct a sofa on a moment's notice

## CELEBRITY PHOTOGRAPHER / PHOTOJOURNALIST

Approachable; adept at making strangers feel comfortable

Finely honed stalking skills

Often found undercover

Not adverse to climbing trees to get that shot

# ART HISTORIAN / MUSEUM CURATOR / GALLERY DIRECTOR

Expert at examining and appraising objects

Comfortable cultivating potential donors

Well-developed aesthetic interests and good taste

Acquires and arranges unusual *objets d'art*

# CAREERS FOR THE CREATIVE INTROVERT (CI)

. . . . . . . . . . . . . . . . . . . . . . . . . . . . . . . .

**CREATIVE INTROVERTS (CIs)** love the finer, more esoteric things in life and tend to take luxury very seriously. CIs enjoy a variety of artistic pursuits, prefer to work independently, and make temperamental collaborators.

Strong career choices for the Creative Introvert include:

RESTAURANT CRITIC / FOOD WRITER

· · · · · · · · · · · · · · · · · · · · · · · · · · · · · · · · · · · · · · · · · · · · ·

ARTIST'S MODEL

· · · · · · · · · · · · · · · · · · · · · · · · · · ·

PERFUMER

· · · · · · · · · · · · · · ·

SPA THERAPIST

· · · · · · · · · · · · · · · · · · · · · ·

JAZZ MUSICIAN

# RESTAURANT CRITIC / FOOD WRITER

Exquisitely discriminating palate

High standards for service and ambience

Able to balance criticism with praise

Can evaluate service, ambience, and value

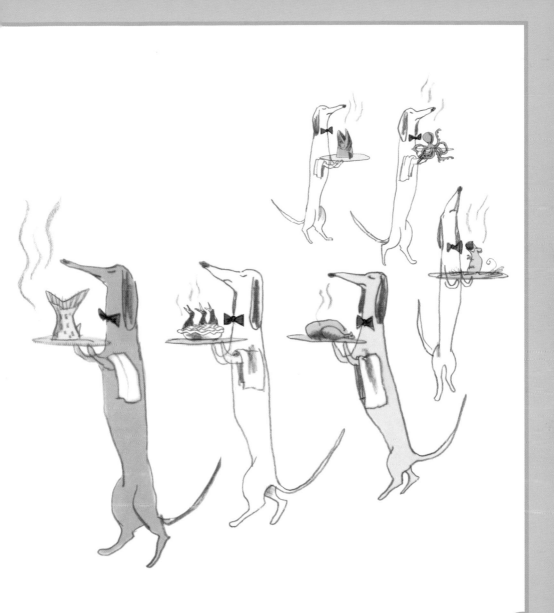

## ARTIST'S MODEL

. . . . . . . . . . . . . . . . . . . . . . . . . . . . . . . .

Can assume many challenging positions

. . . . . . . . . . . . . . . . . . . . . . . . . . . . . . . .

Able to remain motionless for hours

. . . . . . . . . . . . . . . . . . . . . . . . . . . . . . . .

Enjoys playing the roll of muse

. . . . . . . . . . . . . . . . . . . . . . . . . . . . . . . .

Comfortable with nudity

# PERFUMER

Has a discerning nose

Can inhale scents all day without tiring

Tolerates strong odors

Able to identify distinct fragrances

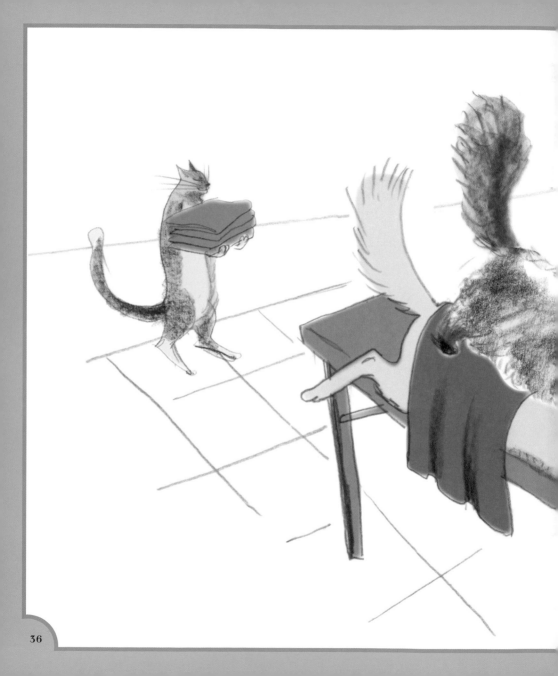

## SPA THERAPIST

No "personal space" issues

Enjoys physical contact

Combines physical stamina
with mental calm

Discreet when called for

# JAZZ MUSICIAN

· · · · · · · · · · · · · · · · · · · · · ·

Interpretive entertainer

· · · · · · · · · · · · · · · · · · · · · · · · · · · ·

Exceptional talent for scat singing

· · · · · · · · · · · · · · · · · · · · · · · · · · · · · · · ·

Comfortable working into the wee hours
of the morning

· · · · · · · · · · · · · · · · · · · · · · · · · · · · · · · ·

Will improvise on other objects if proper
instrument is not available

# CAREERS FOR
# THE LABOR-INTENSIVE
# EXTRAVERT (L-IE)

**LABOR-INTENSIVE EXTRAVERTS (L-IEs)** work hard, play harder, and get by on less sleep than most felines. With energy to spare, L-IEs take pleasure in the element of danger and seek out adventure. Many cats may start out life as L-IEs, changing as they mature.

Perfect career choices include:

STUNT PERFORMER

BARTENDER / CAFÉ BARISTA

MAGICIAN / ILLUSIONIST

PERSONAL TRAINER

XTREME ATHLETE

## STUNT PERFORMER

Ability to fall from great heights
and land on feet

Fearless

Enjoys rough and tumble activities

Motto is "the higher the better"

# BARTENDER / CAFÉ BARISTA

Gregarious, enjoys interacting with the public

Excellent listener

Knows when to serve a milk chaser

Intuits when to cut off a patron and call a cab

## MAGICIAN / ILLUSIONIST

Able to perform sophisticated repertoire
that includes sleight of hand and mentalism

Skilled at making small mammals appear
and disappear at will

Can escape from a closed room

Displays a heightened sense of drama

## PERSONAL TRAINER

Supports fresh interpretation of "weight" training

Pioneering proponent of the low-impact fitness program

Thorough understanding of stretching techniques

Encourages carbo-loading

## XTREME ATHLETE

Bold, hotdogger mentality

Fiercely competitive, plays to win

Good physical shape with
exceptional stamina

Willing to try anything at least once

# CAREERS FOR THE LABOR-INTENSIVE INTROVERT (L-II)

**LABOR-INTENSIVE INTROVERTS (L-IIs)** have excellent dexterity and are "paws-on." They are perfectionists about projects and are used to working alone. L-IIs have the patience to see tasks to a fruitful end.

Excellent career choices include:

PASTRY CHEF

· · · · · · · · · · · · · · · · · · ·

SPORTS COACH

· · · · · · · · · · · · · · · · · · · · · · ·

LANDSCAPE ARCHITECT

· · · · · · · · · · · · · · · · · · · · · · · · · · · · · · · ·

SCULPTOR

· · · · · · · · · · · · · · · ·

PALEONTOLOGIST

# PASTRY CHEF

. . . . . . . . . . . . . . . . . . . . . . . .

Firm, fast kneader

. . . . . . . . . . . . . . . . . . . . . . . .

Enjoys "making biscuits"

. . . . . . . . . . . . . . . . . . . . . . . .

Monitors food quality carefully

. . . . . . . . . . . . . . . . . . . . . . . .

Exhibits steady concentration

## SPORTS COACH

. . . . . . . . . . . . . . . . . . . . . . . . . . . . . . . . .

Possesses exceptional coordination

. . . . . . . . . . . . . . . . . . . . . . . . . . . . . . . . .

Displays superior athletic abilities

. . . . . . . . . . . . . . . . . . . . . . . . . . . . . . . . .

Keeps an eye on slackers and uses
motivational techniques

. . . . . . . . . . . . . . . . . . . . . . . . . . . . . . . . .

A "team player" with a competitive streak

## LANDSCAPE ARCHITECT

· · · · · · · · · · · · · · · · · · · · · · · · · · · · · · · · · · · · · · ·

Thoroughly versed in classical garden design

· · · · · · · · · · · · · · · · · · · · · · · · · · · · · · · · · · · · · · ·

Schooled in the art of feng shui

· · · · · · · · · · · · · · · · · · · · · · · · · · · · · · · · · · · · · · ·

Relies on instinctive, often mystic sensibilities

· · · · · · · · · · · · · · · · · · · · · · · · · · · · · · · · · · · · · · ·

Able to restore harmony and balance in
outdoor surroundings

# SCULPTOR

Excels at carving,
whittling, reshaping

Adept with sharp
pointy instruments

Willing to accept
outdoor commissions

Undaunted by
grandiose ideas

# PALEONTOLOGIST

Carefully inspects and evaluates work

Preoccupation with collecting and assembling
skeletal remains

Specializes in carnivores

Areas of study influenced by ancestral roots

# CAREERS FOR THE INTELLECTUAL EXTRAVERT (IE)

. . . . . . . . . . . . . . . . . . . . . . . . . . . . . . . . . . . . . . . . . . . . . . . . . .

**INTELLECTUAL EXTRAVERTS (IEs)** are strong communicators. Real leaders who keep their eye on the details. IEs have great expectations and as a result can be particular. They are extremely focused and make demands on others in the belief that the end result is worth it. Intellectual Extraverts enjoy being around humans, too.

Ideal career choices include:

CEO

. . . . . . .

POLITICIAN / LOBBIEST

. . . . . . . . . . . . . . . . . . . . . . . . . . . . . . . . . . . . .

SCHOOL TEACHER

. . . . . . . . . . . . . . . . . . . . . . . . . . . . .

EGYPTOLOGIST / ARCHEOLOGIST

. . . . . . . . . . . . . . . . . . . . . . . . . . . . . . . . . . . . . . . . . . .

TV NEWS ANCHOR

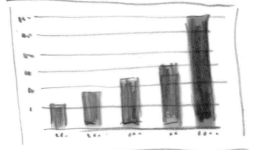

AVIAN CONTROL

## CEO

Keeps an eye on the prize
at all times

Strong leadership skills—
adept at manipulating
subordinates

Forceful—won't take
no for an answer

Clear about needs
and wants

RODENT
DEMOGRAPHICS

# POLITICIAN / LOBBIEST

Knows how to claw his/her way to top

A born meet-and-greeter —always first at the door

Makes a point of knowing everyone in the community,
with an uncanny knack for exerting influence

Extraordinarily gifted at the art of schmoozing

# SCHOOL TEACHER

Generous, nurturing, patient

Imperturbable under virtually any circumstances

Loves children

Eager to demonstrate know-how

# EGYPTOLOGIST / ARCHEOLOGIST

Excavator who relishes the dig

Enjoys fieldwork

Intense study of the cat goddess, Bast

Mastery of the sphinx and its riddles

# TV NEWS ANCHOR

Comfortable in front of a camera

Well-preened and perfectly coiffed

Projects persuasive, trustworthy persona

Anticipates needs of viewing audience

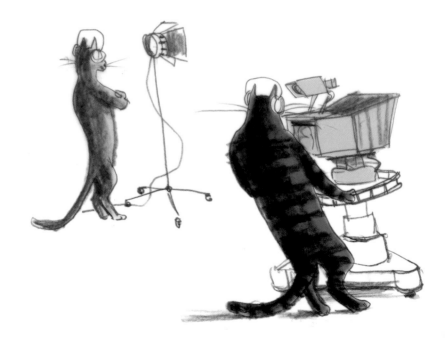

# CAREERS FOR THE INTELLECTUAL INTROVERT (II)

**INTELLECTUAL INTROVERTS (IIs)** are wonks. Abstract thinkers with high IQs, they prefer to work behind the scenes for effective results. They often spend hours in silent reflection, and value quiet and loyalty.

Fulfilling career choices include:

LIBRARIAN

. . . . . . . . . . . . . . .

MARINE BIOLOGIST

. . . . . . . . . . . . . . . . . . . . . . . . . . .

PSYCHOTHERAPIST

. . . . . . . . . . . . . . . . . . . . . . . . . . . .

PRIVATE INVESTIGATOR

. . . . . . . . . . . . . . . . . . . . . . . . . . . . . . . . . .

LEPIDOPTERIST

## LIBRARIAN

Likes to curl up (with a good book)

Often found working on desks and bookshelves

Functions best in quiet environment

Polite and reserved, but not unfriendly

Please be Quiet

73

## MARINE BIOLOGIST

Exhibits knowledge of fish and other aquatic species

Unusual affinity for water

Will catch specimens and conduct tests

Conducts scientific study both before and after catch

# PSYCHOTHERAPIST

Displays capacity for listening to heartfelt confessions

Skilled in fostering relationships

Reveals broad understanding of human emotions

Adept at designing—and implementing—human behavior
modification programs

# PRIVATE INVESTIGATOR

Uncanny ability to blend into surroundings; hides in plain sight

Always alert and observant

Indefatigable—no clue is too insignificant to examine; no lead is too small to follow

Can adopt different personas, disguises, and identities with ease

# LEPIDOPTERIST

Keen tracking and hunting skills

Enjoys exploration and research in the field

Able to spend hours outdoors in motionless observation

Enjoys collecting, categorizing, and displaying
captured specimens

# CAREERS FOR THE INERT INTROVERT (INI)

. . . . . . . . . . . . . . . . . . . . . . . . . . . . . . . . . . . . .

**INERT INTROVERTS (InIs)** are sedentary above all else.
They tend to lack goals and have low ambition.
Enjoy idle pursuits. Not made for jobs requiring
stamina and endurance, or even standing up.

The best—possibly the only—career matches
for InIs are:

SECURITY GUARD

. . . . . . . . . . . . . . . . . . . . . . . . . . . . . .

SOLAR TECHNICIAN

. . . . . . . . . . . . . . . . . . . . . . . . . . . . . .

SOFTWARE ENGINEER

. . . . . . . . . . . . . . . . . . . . . . . . . . . . . .

PRODUCT TESTER

## SECURITY GUARD

Capable of light patrolling, but a
stationary post is preferred

Usually requests the night shift

# SOLAR TECHNICIAN

· · · · · · · · · · · · · · · · · · · · · · · · · · · · · · · · · · · · · · · · · ·

Sets strong example as a passive solar collector

· · · · · · · · · · · · · · · · · · · · · · · · · · · · · · · · · · · · · · · · · ·

Proponent of all alternative energy technologies

# SOFTWARE ENGINEER

Fascination with all tabletop and laptop electronics

Likes to play with mouse, but not always with others

## PRODUCT TESTER

Willing to test the product—day or night

Intolerant of defects

# TIPS FOR ACING
# THE INTERVIEW

· · · · · · · · · · · · · · · · · · · · · · · · · · · · ·

Now that you've identified your cat's career/personality type and chosen the field of endeavor that's right for him or her, it's time to pursue the all-important interview. But before you launch your kitty into a face-to-face meeting with a recruiter or prospective employer, it's wise to have your cat "paws" and review the following points.

## DO

- Assess your presentation—be ruthless.

- Arrive clean and washed. It's best to have performed a full grooming/beauty treatment before your interview.

- Arrive early. If you arrive on time, you're already late

- Keep tail high.

- Be sure your hair is brushed and combed before entering the building.

- Keep nails short and manicured. No one wants to hear clicking, or worse, get scratched.

- Use restroom facility at home.

## BUT

- Do not wear gaudy jewelry or leather collars.

- Do not yawn.

- Do not get caught in bad weather. Set up your transportation to the job. You don't want to look like a drowned rat.

- Do not have anything fishy to eat before the interview.

- Do not ingest catnip within three days of your interview—some firms require on-the-spot drug testing.

- Do not offer a limp paw when greeting the interviewer.

- Do not sit in the interviewer's chair.

- Do not sit in the interviewer's lap.

- Do not play with objects on interviewer's desk.

- Do not touch the interviewer's computer.

- Do not show boredom in any way.

- Do not attempt any personal grooming at any time during the interview.

- Do not rub against the interviewer at anytime.

- Do not show your claws.

- Do not dash into room; move slowly, but with confidence.

- No staring out the window or daydreaming.

- Try not to be contemptuous of the interviewer—he or she does not need to know you can do the job better.

# BE STRONG.

. . . . . . . . . . . . . . . . . . . . . . .

# BE YOURSELF.

# ACKNOWLEDGMENTS

Thank yous go out to so many: My editor Veronica, a lovely Creative Extrovert, who brought joie de vivre to the book and my life and was a pleasure to work with; my book designer, Betsy, for her elegant design; my wonderful publisher, Aaron, who championed the project; and all the folks at Ten Speed Press and Crown Publishing—you guys are the greatest! To Sorche, my incredible agent, (and her charming cat, Hemingway, who introduced us). She totally "got" the book. Her unique talents and intimate understanding of cat behavior were inspiring (I feel so fortunate!). And to Ann—for her delightful illustrations and all around sense of humor. She gave the book soul.

To my dear friends and family (love you!). A special thanks to Mar, what can I say . . . for everything; John-O; Peggy, who convinced the powers that be I should have a kitty or . . . two; Dorrie, Glady, Mark, Em, Joshika, Jake, and Shawn; Loanne; Debbie for support; Frances for your encouragement; Julie and Ellen for letting me borrow The General and Marie; Beverly for helping me get serious; Citrus for believing; Barbara, who gave me that extra kick; and especially Martha, who read the book, made suggestions, and who is there for me in so many ways.

And to Steve, my eternal love, who gave me the gift of time and space and made it all possible.